ALLIGATOR

CRAB

DOLPHIN

KANGAROO

RAT

JELLYFISH

LADYBUG

ANT

BABOON

MONKEY

DUCK

LION

OCTOPUS

SEA TURTLE

ELEPHANT

BIRD

BEAR

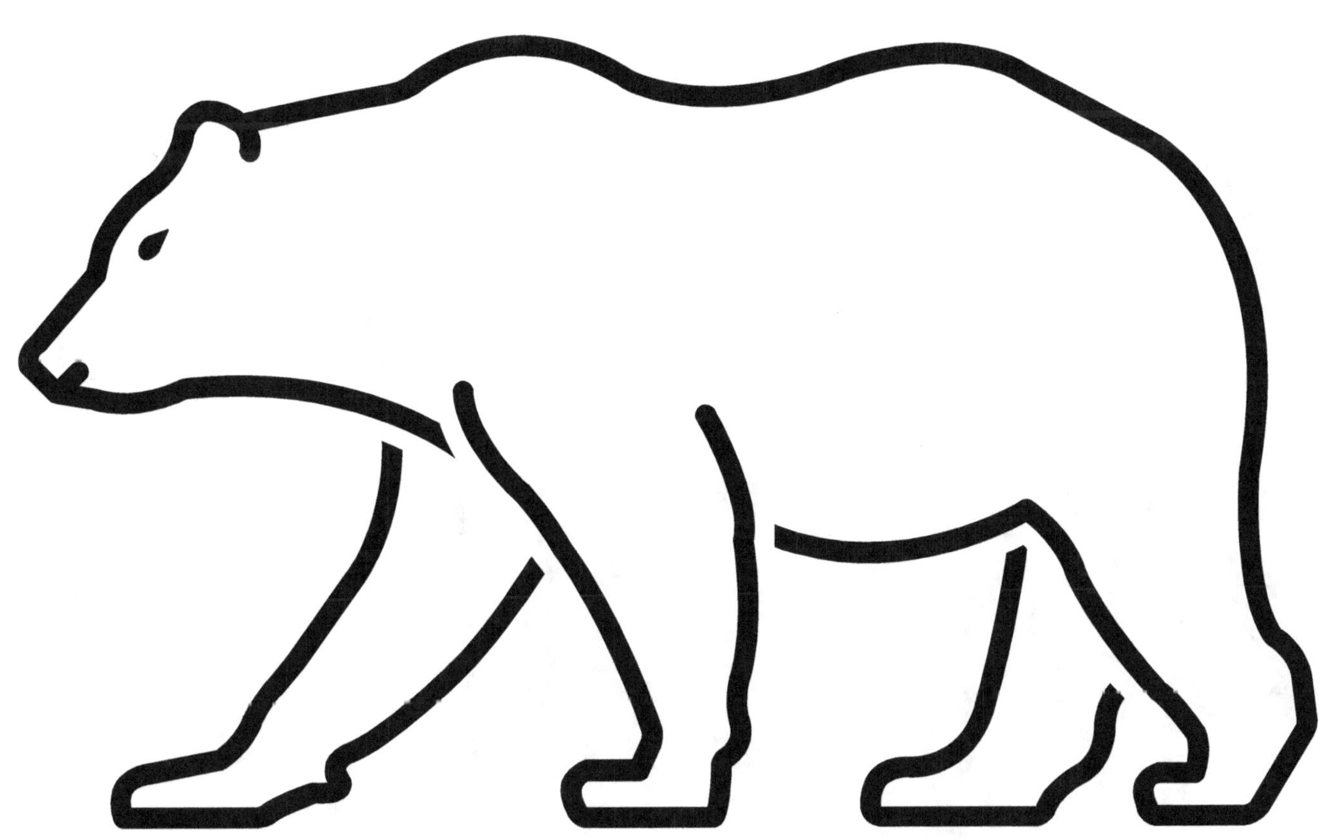

HORSE

PENGUIN

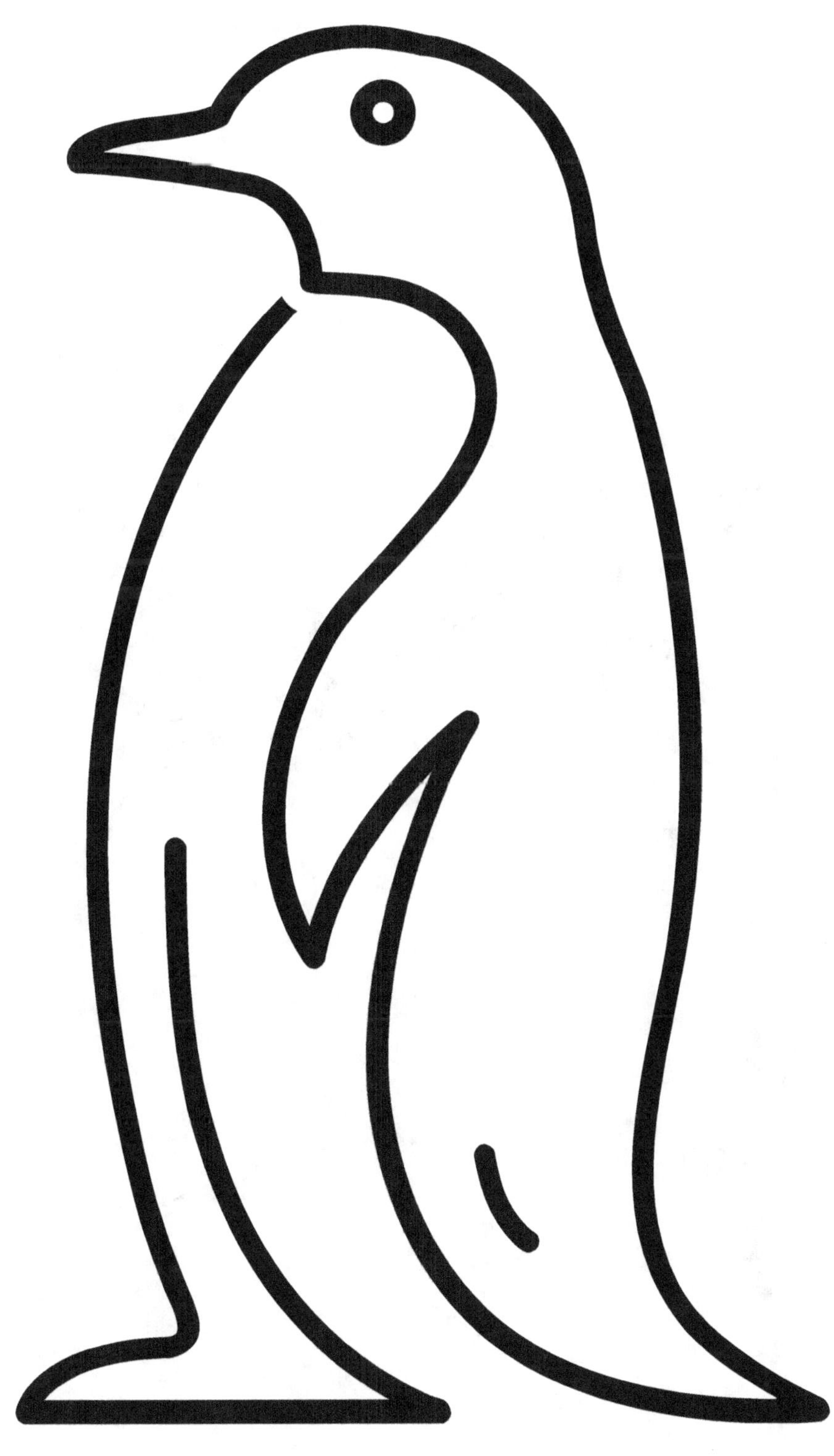

UNICORN

FISH

BEAR

CRAB

CAT

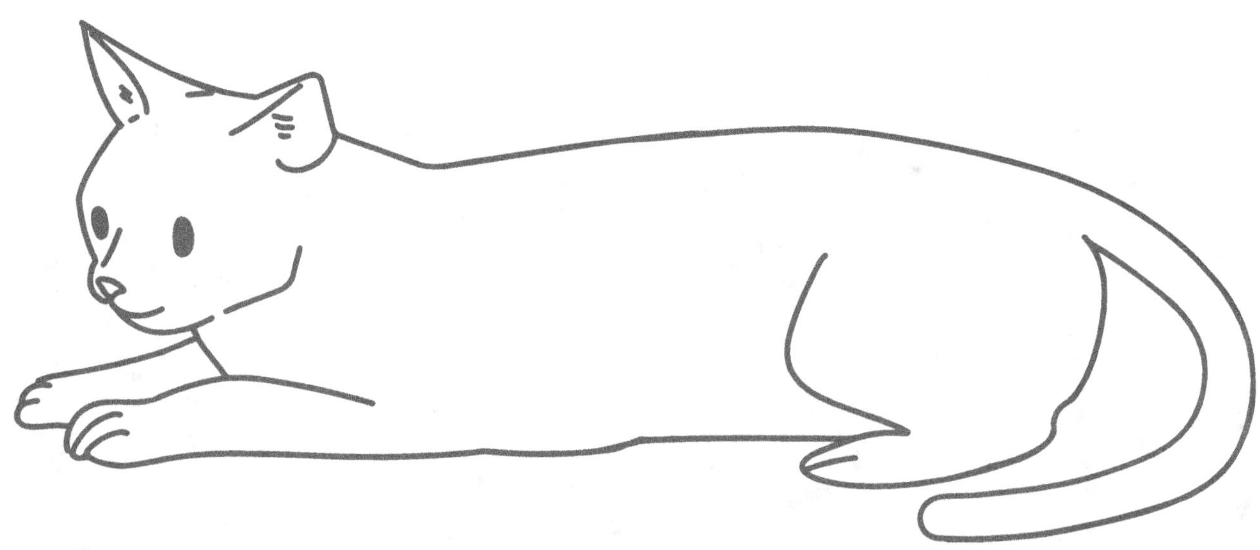

SEA TURTLE

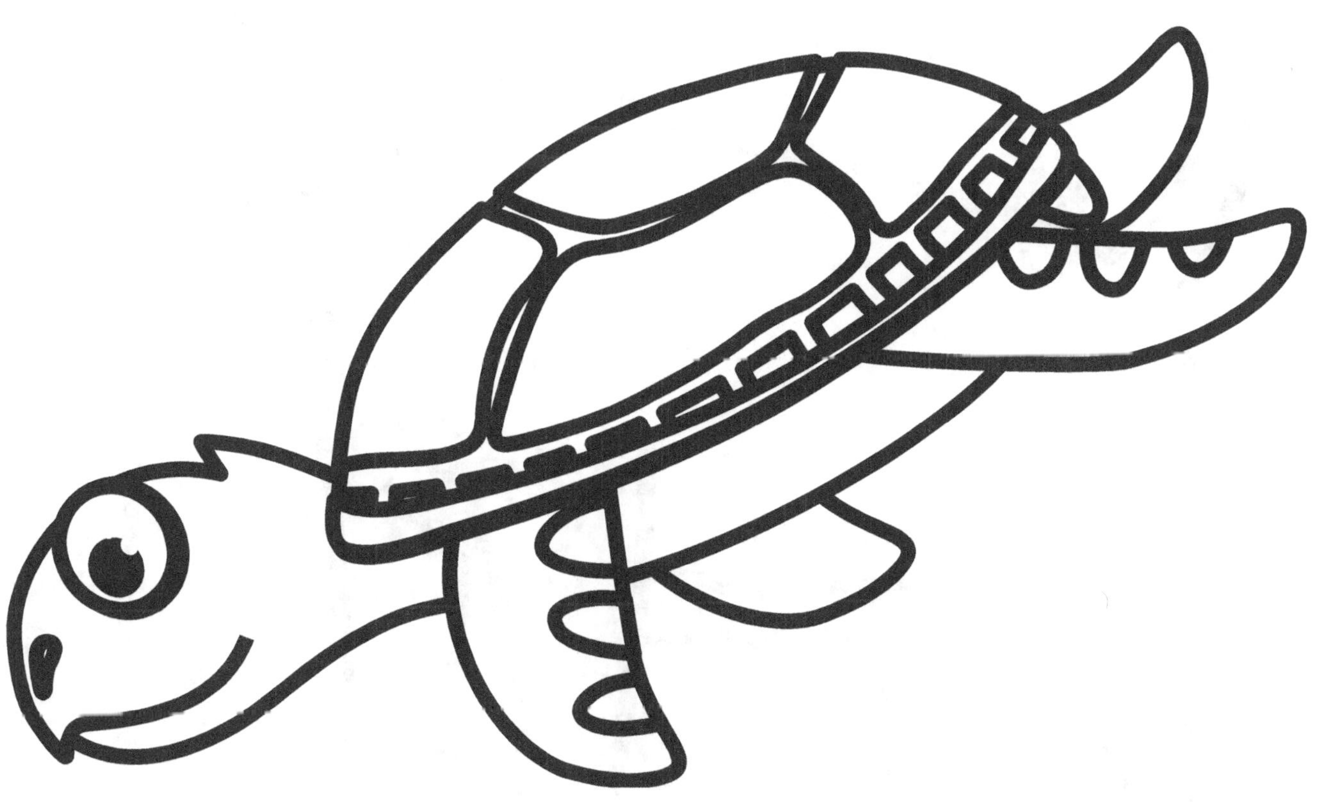

DOG

SEAHORSE

CAT

SEA LION

HERMIT CRAB

SQUID

ZEBRA

LION

FISH

ROOSTER

GIRAFFE

DUCK

TIGER

LIZARD

VULTURE

WILD CAT

YAK

COW

WOLF

ELEPHANT

HORSE

FOX

BEE

BEAR

CAMEL

ANT

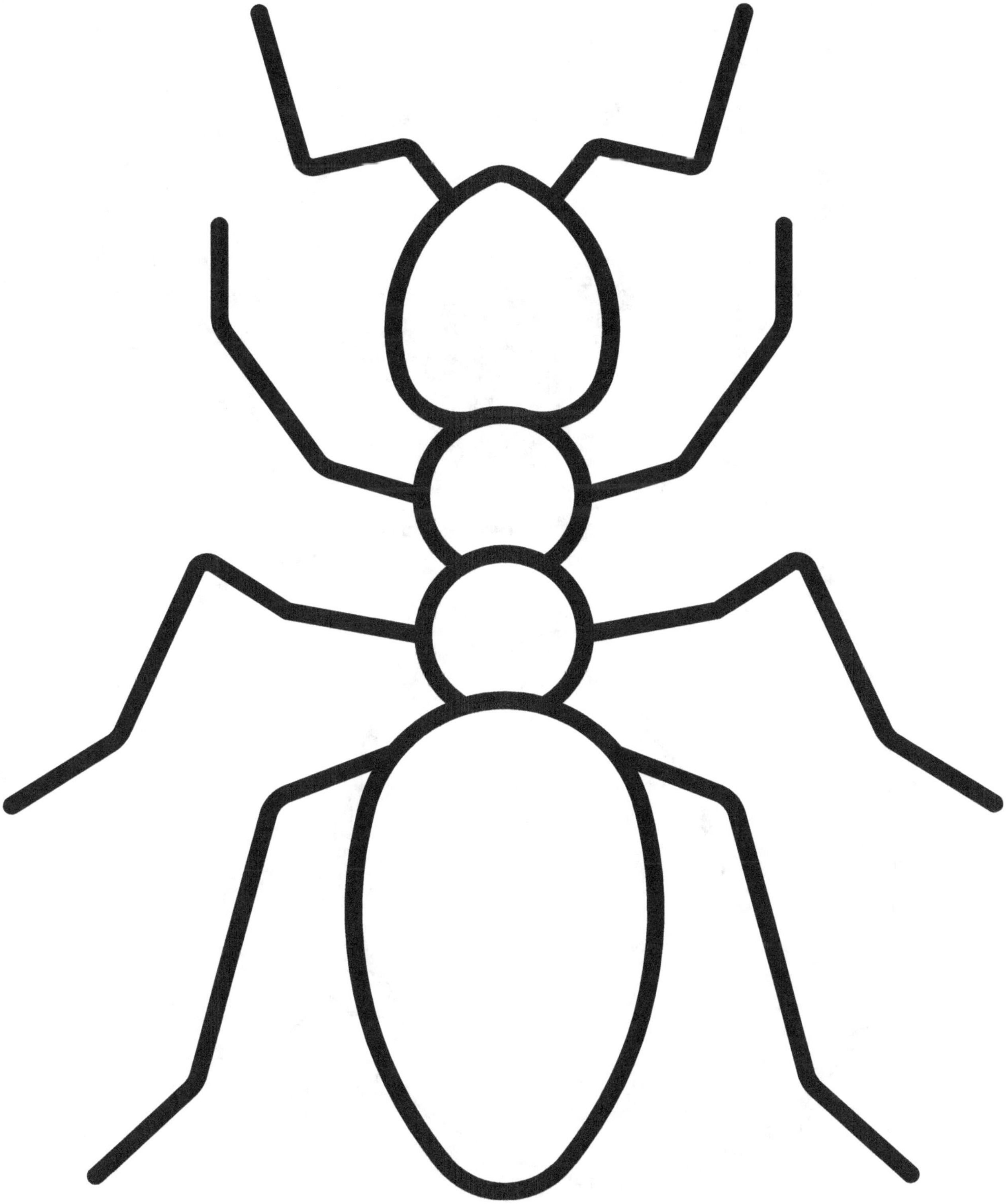

KOALA

GORILLA

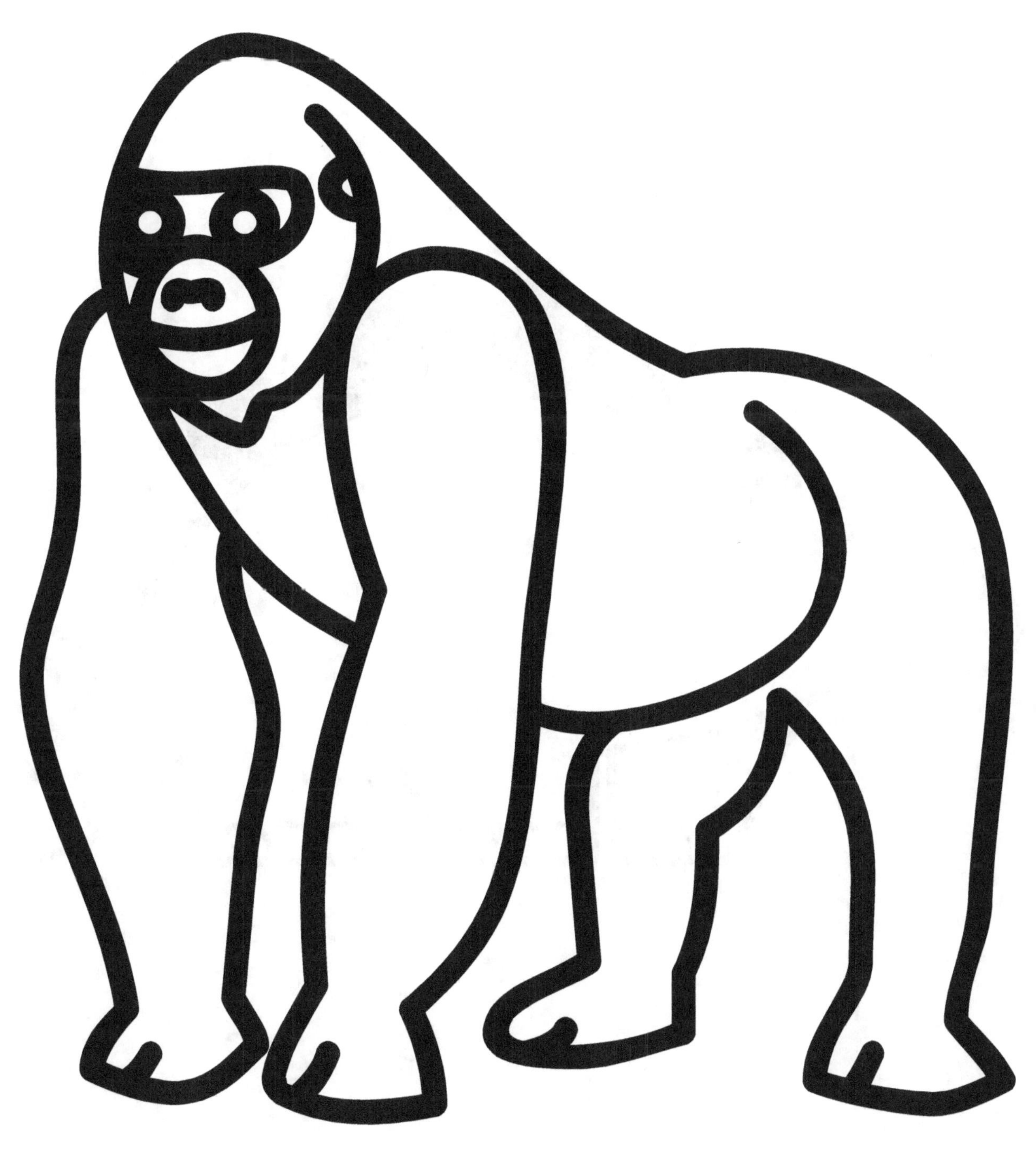

DINOSAUR

INSECT

UNICORN

BEE

BUTTERFLY

SQUIRREL

DEER

RABBIT

TURKEY

OWL

HEDGEHOG

OSTRICH

AARDVARK

PENGUIN

STARFISH

SHARK

FISH

SEAL

BUTTERFLY

PIG

INSECT

CAT

JELLYFISH

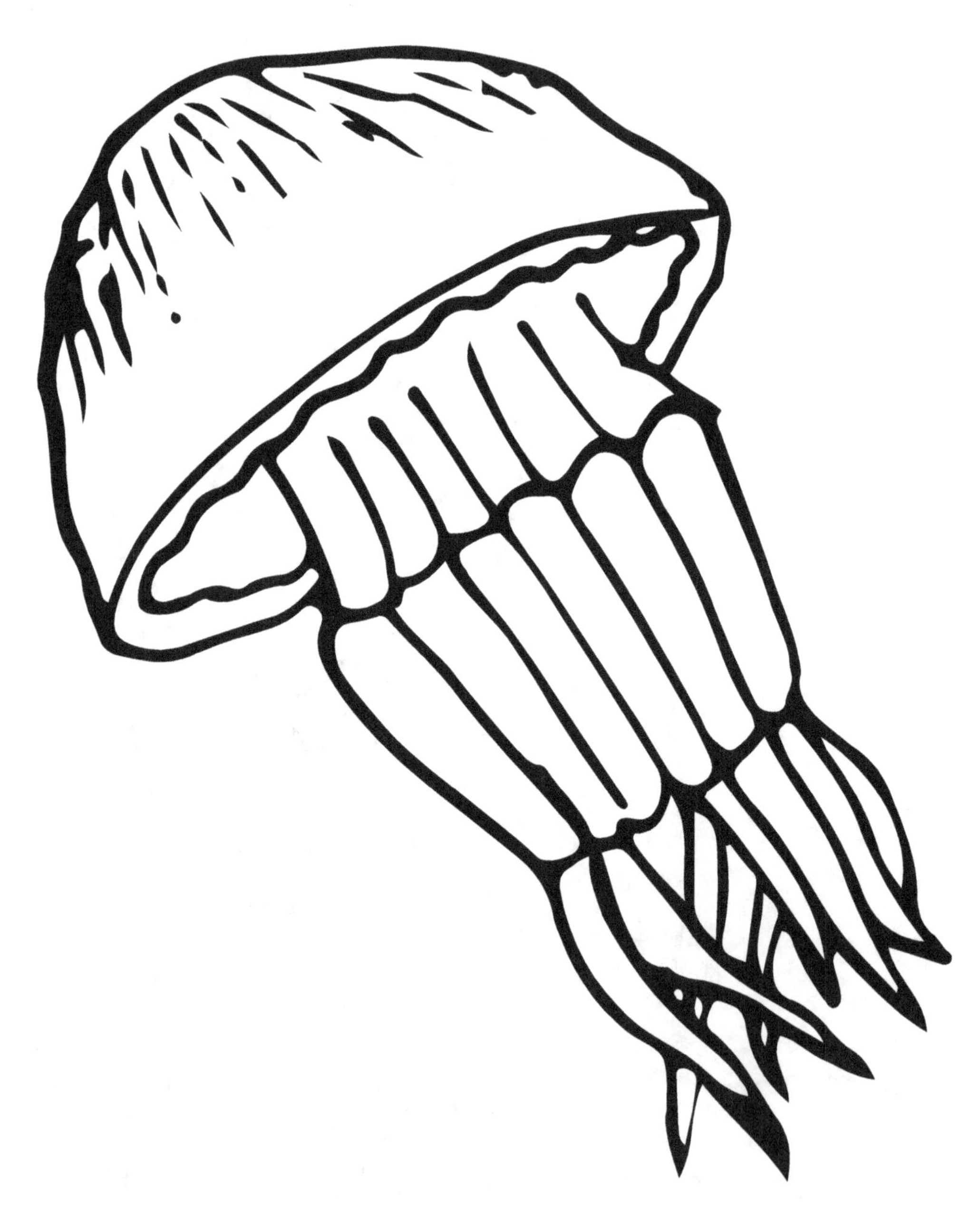

DOG

PARROT

COW

BEAR

INSECT

BUTTERFLY

ANT

RABBIT

CHICK

INSECT

CHICKEN

FISH

PRAWN

PIG

COW

SHEEP

GOAT

FLAMINGO

DEER

SQUIRREL

RACOON

PIG

RACOON

LION